How Can Change?

**by
Mike Downham**

MAPLE
PUBLISHERS

How Can Britain Change?

Author: Mike Downham

Copyright © 2024 Mike Downham

The right of Mike Downham to be identified as author of this work has been asserted by the author in accordance with section 77 and 78 of the Copyright, Designs and Patents Act 1988.

ISBN 978-1-83538-355-1 (Paperback)
   978-1-83538-356-8 (E-Book)

Cover Design and Book Layout by:
  White Magic Studios
  www.whitemagicstudios.co.uk

Published by:
  Maple Publishers
  Fairbourne Drive, Atterbury,
  Milton Keynes,
  MK10 9RG, UK
  www.maplepublishers.com

Acknowledgement

Some of these pieces have been published before in either the Scottish Socialist Party's Voice magazine, or the Scot E3 website. Some have not been published before.

HOW CAN BRITAIN CHANGE?

John Holloway's book *Change The World Without Taking Power* (2002), which starts with a first chapter about *The Scream*, does not refer to *The Scream* (1893), a painting by Edvard Munch. *The Scream* is Munch's most famous work. It has been widely interpreted as representing the universal anxiety of modern man. As Holloway says: "... our scream arises from our negative experience of capitalist society, from the fact that we are oppressed ...". What follows is an explanation of *The Scream*, together with some practical suggestions about what could be changed in British society. It studies changes in health, mental health, health services, food, land, transport, work, global warming, nature, and how to achieve change. It agrees with John Holloway that change can realistically be achieved without taking power.

HEALTH IN SCOTLAND (12.8.19)

"Overweight Scots outnumber smokers 2:1," the *Metro* told us recently. And according to new figures from Cancer Research UK, being overweight trumps smoking as the leading cause of bowel, kidney, ovarian, and liver cancer in Scotland.

Just how much illness is caused by the capitalist market-led economic system (the "Economy of Madness," as Asbjørn Wahl has called it), we won't know until we've replaced that system. But we already know a lot about what the unfettered marketing of fast food, cigarettes, and alcohol has done to Scotland's health. Community mental health teams have become increasingly aware that it's the market-driven stresses of underpaid, insecure, and alienating work that are responsible for the current epidemic of depression and anxiety.

Cancer Research UK has launched a campaign across the UK to increase awareness of the link between obesity and cancer. Another well-intentioned, top-down initiative, unlikely to have much impact because it's focussed on symptoms rather than causes. Worse, it puts responsibility onto overweight people – who are not primarily responsible for the problem.

Blaming people or the NHS for Scotland's poor health record misses the point. In the different, fairer society we're heading for, a whole raft of illnesses will melt away. Keeping that in mind can give us strength in the overall struggle. Not all of us experience daily life as a constant battle with work, benefits, housing, and making ends meet, but every single one of us is a patient. If we don't need a doctor today, we're conscious we may need one tomorrow. Illness is a fact of life – we have that in common.

As for the NHS, there will be less illness for it to deal with in a fairer society, and we have a huge reserve of good practice that we'll be able to draw on. "Stop whinging and get on with it" was more or less what the orthopaedic surgeon said to me at the end of a recent consultation about my arthritic hip. He'd carefully asked how much pain I have, what painkillers I take, how far I can walk, and what the pain stops me from doing. He examined me on the couch, then showed me my X-ray. "You're much too good for surgery, Mike." "Is that because the NHS doesn't have the resources to bother with me?" I asked. "Not a bit of it," he replied. "Hip replacement is a major operation with significant risks." He detailed the risks—specific ones like a shortened leg or dislocation of the new joint, and general ones like anaesthetic complications and superbug infection. "In your case, my opinion is that the risks outweigh the benefits."

I left feeling that this had been a highly satisfactory consultation. Not only do I no longer face the prospect of surgery in the immediate future, but I'd been treated with respect, had my questions fully answered, and had been given the technical reasons for his advice. What's more, the pain in my hip has improved now that I've started to use it more, rather than protect it.

There are, however, improvements that we'll need to make to the NHS. It needs decentralising, democratising, de-privatising, and de-mystifying. All these changes will evolve naturally in a society based on participative democracy and public ownership.

We can learn more about health service organisation from poor countries than from rich ones. In Cuba, one doctor and one nurse live on each block and are responsible for the primary health care of the people who live on that block. In Tanzania, a community health worker is chosen from and by their immediate neighbourhood and given basic training in health promotion and triage of illnesses. In the fairer society we are seeking, elected local health committees, which will design and control health services for the people in their community, in partnership with their health workers, will be able to draw on these Cuban and Tanzanian models, as well as others from across the world.

More problematic will be how to link local services with hospitals. The current link between general practice and hospitals is seriously dysfunctional. It simply doesn't meet most patients' needs. The reasons for this failure are complex and go back a long way. One fundamental problem is the power relationship between doctors and patients. Despite many admirable and hard-working doctors, this power imbalance persists.

Crocodile Dundee had a good angle on the demystification of health professionals. Finding himself at a cocktail party in New York, hedged in by exchanges between the other guests about their progress with their latest psychotherapists, he famously contributed, "In Walkabout Creek, if you have a problem, you tell Wally. Wally tells everyone. End of problem."

The practical point is that our health, along with the efficiency of its health services, could be greatly enhanced if doctors and patients learned to work together in a more balanced partnership. One step towards this is to provide lifelong opportunities for people to learn about illnesses. More confident and less deferential patients would contribute more to consultations, which would become more effective diagnostically, quicker, and less often necessary—especially if general practices are structured so that doctors and patients get to know each other in the way they used to in the early days of the NHS. Changes in these directions would also reduce the need for investigations. The current explosion of tests is largely due to doctors not knowing their patients and not having time to exercise their clinical skills of history-taking and physical examination. It's quicker and easier to order another scan. Referral to a hospital specialist would be less often necessary too. When it's necessary, the patient will be able to bridge the current information gap between the two arms of the service.

CHILD CARE, VIRUSES, AND CLIMATE (29.1.19)

One of the impacts of climate change not much talked about is that it will throw new illnesses at us. This isn't just a future possibility—it's already happening. The horrifying 2014-15 Ebola virus epidemic in West Africa, for example. And all the virus infections we're experiencing these days, especially in young children, are probably linked to climate change too. Certainly, people are saying there are more of them, that they are worse, and that they take longer to clear up. Warmer winters are on the side of viruses, helping them to get past our immune defences and to spread themselves more widely.

At the B&Q checkout the other day, the cashier asked me if I'd had a good Christmas. Not exactly, I told her, because I'd had the flu. She said there had been lots of nasty bugs celebrating Christmas in her neighbourhood too, some causing the flu, some coughs and colds, some D&V. She reckoned it had to do with all the children needing to be cared for outside families these days. Most parents, she said, even if there are two of them, struggle to make ends meet, having to work more and more hours between them. I reckon she was right.

More Children Being Cared For

The proportion of families who rely on others to care for their children—whether it's grandparents, free nursery places, or paid care—has exploded over the last generation. And children are starting some form of child care at a younger age these days. On top of pre-school children, there are all those four-year-olds at school. Once we have fought our way to a fairer society, we will look back on the way we put 25 of our precious four-year-olds into a room with one teacher, even with the support of a classroom assistant, as one of the craziest things we ever did. It's not only the number of children the teacher has to deal with; it's also that many of them are, to a lesser or greater extent, disturbed, largely as a result of having lost the consistency of care that only parents and local communities can give. Do four-year-olds really need formal education? Surely what they need are opportunities to play safely and creatively, and chances to explore the world around them, particularly the natural world. A trainee teacher told me recently that she took some kindling sticks into the classroom for the kids to build structures with, and one of the lads, picking up a stick, asked, "Miss, is this real wood?"

Teachers, Classroom Assistants, and Child Care Workers

Teachers and classroom assistants are being asked by the state to do the impossible and, into the bargain, are being paid a pittance for their trouble. So are workers in child care. It's good to see that all these workers, often at the end of their tethers, are now standing up to say, "Enough!" We should give our full support in whatever way we can to these protests by some of the most important workers in society.

Viruses

But what are we to do about these viruses—the viruses that infest our schools, nurseries, and child-care establishments? They spread to parents and, worse, to grandparents. And, of course, teachers, assistants, and carers usually catch them too. The overall impact in terms of suffering, stress, and time off work is huge. Instead of just grinning and bearing all this, could we get more clued-up about these infections and about how they spread? Then, something to reduce cross-infection might follow.

Hard-Pressed Doctors

The NHS, despite the expertise, commitment, and kindness of its workers, will increasingly fail to meet our needs due to the choices our politicians continue to make—starving the service of money and controlling it centrally through bureaucrats. As a result, doctors and nurses are becoming more and more hard-pressed. Moreover, there are nowhere near enough newly trained doctors going into general practice—they don't like the look of the workload.

Learning About Illnesses

So let's start, collectively, to take back some responsibility for our health needs by learning more about how to better manage illnesses ourselves. We've fallen into the habit, I suggest, of thinking that only professionals with extensive training can help us when we're ill. But a lot of it isn't rocket science. We can learn a great deal simply by sharing each other's experiences of illness. Within any person's social network, there's likely to be someone who has had experience with most common illnesses, either personally or through the experience of a family member or friend. We can learn from each other, for example, how to spot virus infections earlier, how to best look after children who catch them, how they don't always need to be seen by a doctor, what signs to look for of bacterial infections that should alert us to see the doctor, and how viruses spread.

We may be surprised by just how much we can usefully learn about illnesses in general. We can begin to see ourselves not as passive patients, but as partners working with the experts.

A NEW NARRATIVE FOR THE PANDEMIC AND THE FUTURE (22.10.20)

It's hard to choose which of the government's approaches to Covid has been the most scandalous. We could point to the Home Office's kettling of refugees and asylum seekers into hotels: a man who fled to the UK 20 years ago, settled in Glasgow, and became an energetic advocate for refugees and asylum seekers in Scotland, described this as a worse experience for the people rounded up than the camps in Calais or Lesbos. Or we could focus on the mass discharging of older people from hospitals into care homes at the peak of the epidemic, with its devastating effects on thousands of older people and on the care workers who did their very best for these people as they died. Or we could highlight the appalling failure to address the special risks faced by BAME workers—such as the 35 deaths of London bus drivers, which finally prompted them to seal up their front doors and refuse to take fares, prioritising their safety in the face of government inaction.

At the root of these and other catastrophic impacts of government policies is the absence of a virus elimination strategy. And let's be clear: the Scottish Government's approach has been no different in substance from the UK Government's—the only difference has been in presentation. Instead of eliminating the virus, both governments were prepared to sacrifice members of large sections of the working class—the retired, the Black, those with chronic ill-health and disabilities, the unemployed, and refugees and asylum seekers—in what has proved to be a completely futile attempt to protect the economy. Two things about this strategy are now glaringly obvious: it's deeply unfair, and it doesn't work.

It doesn't work because it's bad science. The science isn't highly technical; it's common sense. We've known from the start that this virus is unusual in that it affects different groups of people in widely differing ways. It's both a killer and yet has a negligible impact on others, especially children and young people, who can carry it without being aware of it. It stands to reason that if you open up some sectors of society while keeping others closed, and only close down those sectors in some parts of a small, densely populated country, the virus will spread whenever two people speak to each other at less than two metres' range. What is being called a "lockdown" even now, the second time around, isn't a proper lockdown at all—it's partial, often arbitrary, and always too late.

We've also known from the start that this virus was highly unlikely to result in long-term immunity for those who catch it. Immunity will probably last for a year at most. This makes the idea of herd immunity, which still drives government policy, utterly daft in the absence of a vaccine.

So, the first strand of our new Covid narrative has to be more complete and nation-wide lockdowns, with adequate compensatory funding for workers until the virus has been eliminated. Along with this, we should insist that the Test and Trace system be brought fully into the NHS. It will never be effective if it's driven by profit.

If science is to be beneficial to human society and the planet, it must be based on common sense and rational thinking. Working-class people can make informed and critical use of scientific knowledge if they come together to make sense of how the world works and to find solutions to problems collectively, calling on the opinions of experts as necessary. The notion that we can't just leave science to the experts has become brutally clear in this pandemic, in which the government has co-opted a handful of experts to give it the advice that suits its ideology and political agenda. We should be proud that in the UK, a strong group of scientists has emerged who are not standing for this. They set up their own Independent SAGE committee, which meets in public, involves workers and communities in its deliberations, publishes its findings quickly and in plain language, and has an excellent website—see, for example, the six-minute clip of a Channel 4 interview with two members of Independent SAGE last week - https://www.independentsage.org/christina-pagel-discussing-tiered-restrictions-on-good-morning-britain/.

The Independent SAGE is a model of how experts and the public should interact, making knowledge the property of all.

We would do well to stop using the debased term "lockdown" altogether and replace it, perhaps, with "keeping each other safe." The word "lockdown," with its prison origin, is highly authoritarian and contrary to public health principles. Telling people what to do, passing new legislation, and threatening them with fines will only work with some people. Others, as we've seen, just won't or can't comply, and you don't need many of these to keep the virus happy. Good public health practice has recognised this for at least 150 years, going back to the cholera epidemics in Glasgow. People needed to be personally encouraged and materially supported to do the socially responsible thing. And they needed to trust that the local public health workers' advice was reliable.

Last week, the government put a lot of effort into failing to bribe the Mayor of Greater Manchester to comply with its centrally imposed so-called severe lockdown. How can anyone trust a government that desperate to impose its authority?

Trust is fundamental in an epidemic—not only trust in safety advice but also trust in each other. This means trying to understand where people are coming from when they aren't sticking to the advice, rather than leaping to blame them. Young people are bound to want to get together—it's an inextricable part of being young, I seem to remember. We need to invest in ways to make socialising possible for them that aren't a threat to collective safety. Instead, faced with demonisation, some of them have been chased away to join far-right conspiracy-theorist groups.

Our new narrative should also include a strand of what we could call "local control." Although we generally need much stricter safety measures in workplaces, schools, colleges, the hospitality sector, and on public transport, each neighbourhood will require different measures, depending, for example, on what their particular schools are like in terms of class size, class space, and ventilation. Workplaces where residents of different neighbourhoods are employed will vary in terms of safety, as will the public transport they need to travel to work. Above all, there will be local differences in the level of infection at different times, which each community can consider. It was all these factors that local public health workers considered during epidemics before the service was hollowed out and centralised. We need to fight to get those local services back, but in the meantime, we'll have to do much of it ourselves through neighbourhood COVID committees, who would also be able to watch out for people in their community needing particular support, whether material or emotional.

What becomes clear is that the narrative we need to get through this pandemic—a narrative based on knowledge, fairness, trust, local control, and working together—is much the same narrative we need for the future. The left has lacked a coherent proactive narrative for the best part of 50 years. We've been battered by the onslaught of neoliberal capitalism into just reacting, which assumes powerlessness. Part of the problem is that the right has successfully twisted our language to the extent that we've been stuck for words with which to communicate our vision. They've twisted socialism into Stalinist communism, public ownership into Clause 4 nationalisation, state regulation into stifling enterprise, support for Palestine into antisemitism, democracy into the current sham of parliamentary democracy, and revolution into chaos.

By the time this piece goes to press, we will have been thrown into a second wave of infection, with all its likely devastation. The excess deaths figure for the UK from March 23rd to May 31st was 63,596. The second wave will bring another slaughter, and for those who survive: further poverty, further unemployment, and further mental distress. For all of this, the government is squarely to blame.

But people in Scotland have begun to say "enough is enough," as recently demonstrated by the Black Lives Matter campaign, with its sights now set on ending all racism in Scotland, and by the Council Cuts campaigns for new and better services, not just opposing cuts. We may not be able to stop the second wave, but there are realistic ways for us to reduce its scale, mitigate its impacts, and at the same time organise for a better future.

The pandemic has given us two unique opportunities—first, to fill the pandemic narrative vacuum with a narrative of our own, including what safety we need, what services we want, and an end to racism in Britain. And second, to articulate that narrative, both now for COVID-19 and beyond for a different future, in words that all working-class people can immediately relate to. If we speak of safety, knowledge, fairness, trust, local control, and change, and if we stay together rather than retreating into our sectarian silos, we can win back the high ground and make sure we don't go back to the way it was before.

A BOTCHED REHEARSAL (4.12 21)

It's been nearly two long years since we first began to grasp the potential scale and danger of this new virus. At that point, some prescient individuals suggested that our reaction to the pandemic would serve as a rehearsal for our performance in the forthcoming big show of climate breakdown.

This wasn't the first time the term 'rehearsal' had been used in the context of leftist organisation. John Berger described every act of resistance as a rehearsal. Colin Barker titled his 1987 book *Revolutionary Rehearsals*, documenting the uprisings in France, Chile, Portugal, Iran, and Poland between 1968 and 1980. He used the title again in his subsequent book *Revolutionary Rehearsals in the Neoliberal Age*, written jointly with Gareth Dale and Neil Davidson and published this year—posthumously for both Colin and Neil—which describes the uprisings in Eastern Europe, South Africa,

Indonesia, Argentina, Bolivia, Venezuela, Sub-Saharan Africa, and Egypt since 1989.

It's reasonable, I think, to say that we've made a right mess of the COVID rehearsal. Had we known two years ago what we know today, we would have learned our lines and cues more thoroughly. What we know today is that 9,634 people in Scotland have died; the majority of these snuffed-out lives have been among the poor, the disabled, and the marginalised; that 99,000 people in Scotland are living with Long COVID; that about 10% of children who catch the virus go on to suffer disabling poor health for weeks or months; and that the NHS has broken down.

That the NHS has actually broken down—no longer just something we feared might happen—was brought home to me this week by hearing about a middle-aged woman in the Paisley area with an 18-month history of severe neck pain. She waited so long for surgery that she was forced to give up her job as a care worker and then lost her home because she couldn't keep up with her mortgage repayments. And this is not the only tragic story of NHS failure we could share among us.

Now, the Omicron variant (whether or not it turns out to be as bad as feared—we'll need to wait a week or so before we know) is shouting at us from the wings, warning that if we allow the virus to spread—whether in Scotland's communities, schools, and workplaces among an incompletely vaccinated population, or in largely unvaccinated countries that have been pushed to the back of the queue because they can't afford vaccines—we will inevitably face a variant that evades current vaccines.

The cues were there in the script from the beginning. Had we read and understood them, we would have known that we couldn't trust the governments of wealthy countries, including Scotland, to rely solely on vaccines or to prioritise supplying and reducing the cost of vaccines for poorer nations. These governments are locked into a system where profit trumps health. Yesterday's top news featured Pfizer gleefully suggesting that annual vaccinations might be necessary— without addressing the financial and logistical nightmare of vaccinating eight billion people every year. Pfizer is not only anticipating a limitless market but also revelling in having outperformed AstraZeneca both technically and in terms of propaganda.

Just as profit trumps health, allowing the COVID virus to spread, it also trumps the devastating impacts of global heating that are unfolding for all humanity. COP26 has made it abundantly clear that neither wealthy governments nor the oil and gas corporations are prepared to take effective action against global heating, despite being fully aware of and no longer denying the scale of the impacts resulting from their inaction.

How can it be that a small fraction of human beings can inflict such suffering on the rest of their species? Andreas Malm and colleagues, in their new book *White Skin, Black Fuel*, try to explain:

> *They are not perturbed by the smell of blazing trees. They do not worry about the sight of sinking islands; they do not run from the roar of approaching hurricanes; their fingers never need to touch the stalks of withered harvests; their mouths do not become sticky and dry after a day with nothing to drink … After the past three decades, there can be no doubt that the ruling classes are constitutionally incapable of responding to the catastrophe in any other way than by expediting it; of their own accord, under their inner compulsion, they can do nothing but burn their way to the end.*

As we receive our final call to take the stage in the climate crisis, what have we learned from the Covid rehearsal? What are our lines, and what are our most critical cues?

The best approach to these questions may be to first examine what mistakes we made in the rehearsal to avoid repeating them. We should perhaps beware of:

- Knocking politely on town hall and parliament doors, asking politicians to do things few of them can even contemplate.

- One-off marches and protests that aren't part of a well-charted programme of resistance.

- Loosely knit coalitions that dilute militancy with compromise.

- Hoping to build a social democratic party that could win at the ballot box.

- Organising strictly within our political silos, whether parliamentary parties, revolutionary groups, or single-issue institutions.

- Underestimating the extent to which the ruling classes have stifled trade union power, so that the collective withdrawal of labour is no longer the readily available weapon it used to be.

How, then, can we organize if not in these ways? First, the Covid pandemic is far from over—in fact, it can be said to be at a critical point, with the prospect that vaccines may not protect us and that relying on vaccines alone is not sustainable. We'll only be able to overcome this pandemic through traditional public health measures, delivered through a greatly expanded and well-resourced public health service. This is what we should start turning our attention to and fighting for. Covid offers us the experience of another rehearsal, with the key changes needed to address both Covid and climate becoming increasingly clear—the same changes, such as rolling out and investing heavily in existing technologies instead of switching to uncertain ones. Vaccination alone becomes the equivalent of Carbon Capture and Storage: both are profitable for the ruling classes but disastrous for the rest of us.

Second, COP26 has shown us that targeted and sustained direct action works. The Indian farmers, after a year's disruptive presence in Delhi, during which 700 of them died at the hands of the police, have won a historic victory. The first thing Modi did when he returned from Glasgow was announce that he would withdraw the three laws against which the farmers had been protesting. Two weeks later, Shell announced that it was giving up its ten-year plan to extract oil and gas from the Cambo field. This is a huge victory for the Stop Cambo! campaign—a direct result of its persistent visibility in Westminster over the last year and its strong performance at COP in Glasgow.

However, amidst our celebrations of these two wins, we can see that the farmers continue to swamp Delhi. They want to see the three laws actually withdrawn, not just hear a promise. It is probable that even then they will continue their protest for further, more systemic changes. Stop Cambo! knows it must not relax. There's still Siccar Point Energy to unseat (the majority partner in the development of the Cambo field), and there's the UK Government to force into a decision that no extraction license will be granted. A win is the cue to increase the strength of a protest, not to end it.

Third, we would do well at this point to start discussing what we have so far shunned: how are we to oppose the state oppression that is bound to escalate in response to increased direct action? Is XR right to remain adamant about non-violence, or did Mandela have a point when he said, "The attacks of the wild beast cannot be averted with only bare hands"?

MENTAL HEALTH (30.8.20)

It's not who you are, it's what's been done to you

It's not like breaking your leg

Human distress has become medicalised

Human distress has become commodified

At an online meeting about mental distress during the Covid pandemic, the psychologist introducing the discussion had only been speaking for a few minutes when he suddenly lost his internet connection. The 22 participants paused for a few reflective moments, then took over the meeting. The speaker was never seen or heard from again.

This was an alarming experience for some at the time, but it was also an iconic one, pointing to a crucial question: How much do people experiencing mental distress need the help of experts?

The Biomedical Model of 'Mental Illness'

With the discovery of lithium in 1949, followed quickly by other psychoactive drugs, drug treatment based on ever-changing lists of medical diagnoses has dominated the treatment of people with mental health issues across the world. Pharmaceutical companies, quick to see the potential for profit, developed an effective mix of marketing, distortion of research through funding, and influencing policy documents through corruption of the psychiatrists responsible for drawing them up, notably the DSM (the Diagnostic and Statistical Manual of Mental Disorders). As a result of this institutionalised exploitation, many people who seek or are forced into treatment for mental distress have become locked into drugs and their side effects, sometimes for life, and need constant or frequent care and protection. Of those who manage to return to some sort of normality, most remain highly vulnerable to stress. Psychotherapy has progressively become something only available privately for those who can afford it. On top of this, the introduction, marketing, and promotion of psychoactive drugs have been responsible for a huge epidemic of drug abuse.

Causes of Mental Distress

The diagnosis-led biomedical model of mental distress is finally under effective attack. An alternative symptom-led model is being developed through practice and research, which argues that all mental distress is primarily psychosocial, not biochemical. Human beings' reactions to life events are infinitely variable across a continuous spectrum. People aren't vulnerable; they are made vulnerable. And they are made vulnerable primarily through the power relationships within society. Here's a link to a podcast about the symptom-led model, which you may find worth the hour you need to give to it: https://www.madintheuk.com/2019/09/peter-kinderman-why-we-need-a-revolution-in-mental-health-care/. It's an argument that makes intuitive sense to many sufferers and to many of those who try to help them. The new approach consists first in creating a trusting relationship—not easy for many sufferers whose experiences have made it difficult for them to trust. In that relationship, the aim is to listen carefully to the person's description of their symptoms and to help them identify the main experiences that have led them to feel as they do. Since the key experiences vary widely—employment, debt, housing, personal relationships, loss, racism, school, illness or fear of illness, physical or sexual violence, or even the absurdities of the modern world—what we need to offer is a wide range of specific advice and support for whatever leading issues they identify. These services need to be free and as local as possible, as people in distress and who have lost trust often won't feel able to travel to a service outside their area.

It's important to stress, though, that some people find it hard to relinquish the medical diagnosis they've been encouraged to accept, especially if they have suffered deeply for a long time. They may feel that a diagnosis of, say, depression, bipolar disorder, or schizophrenia has given them the caring attention they need in the loneliness of their suffering. This is understandable, but it can be suggested to them that there are alternative ways of looking at how they feel.

Many people who have been on treatment with psychoactive drugs, perhaps for many years, and have experienced at least some relief from their distress through taking these drugs, will be reluctant to risk a new approach. The symptom-led approach has been described as "tearing up 60 years of psychiatry." It's certainly revolutionary, but all revolutions, if they are to be successful, need to consider some groups of people for whom sudden, specific change isn't easy, however much they may long for change in general. For example, people with sons or daughters who have emigrated to Canada, Australia, or New Zealand may fully understand that air travel must be drastically and quickly reduced to avoid catastrophic global warming. However, it won't be easy for them to stop, or be stopped from flying to visit their children and grandchildren.

Experiences of Mental Distress During the Pandemic

Most of the participants at the recent meeting were able to share their personal experiences of mental distress since the start of the pandemic, despite the remote context of a Zoom meeting. However, it was noticeable that only 50% of those who had registered for the meeting actually attended.

Additionally, two participants who did join later confided that they had not felt able to speak about their feelings. This suggests that remote meetings are not an inclusive method for expressing often painful feelings in a group where most participants have not met each other before.

Those living alone reported that lockdown had been extremely difficult, especially for those who were already struggling with mental distress before the pandemic. Their opportunities for social contact were suddenly removed, often with nothing to replace them. However, some mutual aid groups went beyond food distribution by phoning people living alone on a weekly basis, chatting with them, inquiring about their well-being, and offering assistance.

One participant described how her mental health began to deteriorate in January. Shortly after the lockdown began, she developed extreme anxiety with delusions and was admitted to a psychiatric hospital under a Section. While in the hospital, she started writing poems about her experiences. She read two of her poems during the discussion, and a selection of her poems can be found here: https://www.scribd.com/document/470989297/Poems-by-Leila-Platt-pdf.

It was pointed out that women seemed to have taken on the major part of home-schooling for their children while schools were closed. For some women, the combination of working full-time from home and trying to home-school their children had been very stressful.

For some people, the uncertainty following the relaxation of lockdown measures was equally or more difficult. Returning to 'normal' was fine for those whose sense of normalcy did not involve increased social isolation. While the majority were relieved, individuals experiencing mental distress, especially those living alone, were left with the same sense of isolation and difference. Returning to work, for those who still had jobs, has proven particularly challenging, with no allowances made in the regulations for people experiencing mental distress.

Some participants agreed with the suggestion that the stigma of mental distress—an ongoing challenge for sufferers—had, to some extent, dissolved during the pandemic, replaced by a sense of solidarity. Now that everyone was experiencing anxiety, there was a feeling of shared experience. However, some felt that this sense of solidarity had disappeared with the relaxation of lockdown measures. Others questioned the validity of comparing the anxiety experienced during the pandemic and its economic and social impacts with their own longer-term and deeper experiences of distress. There were even surprising suggestions that people with experience of long-term mental distress were better equipped to cope with lockdown. It was suggested that some of the differences in reactions to stigma or solidarity might be attributed to variations between communities.

Variability

We need to be wary, one participant pointed out, of any approach to mental distress that does not consider the wide variability both in how people experience distress and in the origins of their distress. Any attempt to lump people into groups is unlikely to be helpful. For some individuals, there may be just one unique issue contributing to their distress. As with all differences, we need to try to understand where people who think or behave differently from us are coming from, rather than blame them. For example, people were blamed for panic shopping at the start of the epidemic. What is and what isn't 'normal'? People react to the challenges that human life inevitably brings in a continuous spectrum of different ways.

The Government

What happened in care homes was described as heart-breaking—so many older people died without their children at their side, which was devastatingly confusing for those with dementia. There will be a 'tsunami' of grief among the children and partners of those who died, whether in care homes or hospitals—grief exacerbated if they were unable to be present in those last days and hours. The Government was seen as wholly responsible for the appalling experiences of both residents and staff in care homes; it was considered a crime.

The Government had been ready to put our mental health at risk as well as our physical health. In capitalist society, if you cross a line by not 'pulling your weight,' you are seen as unworthy of support. When one group calls for special support, such as people with mental distress, governments fear that everyone will.

Drug Treatment

Several participants shared their experiences with being prescribed SRIs (Serotonin Reuptake Inhibitors). Packaged as safe, these drugs were seen as having become what ECT (Electroconvulsive Therapy) was for previous generations—brutal, often not effective or only effective in the short term, and systemically disempowering. Sometimes, SRIs had produced side effects that significantly increased distress, such as insomnia and loss of appetite. They have been banned in the U.S. due to a surge in suicides among people under 25 taking SRIs. Despite these issues, it often proved difficult to persuade doctors to stop SRIs, even when sufferers reported severe side effects.

One participant described how a strike during lockdown in a French factory producing mood stabilisers made it impossible for him to renew his prescription. He quickly began to feel better and has not used them since.

In general, it was thought that drugs for anxiety and depression are used in the hope of providing quick fixes to get people back to work, saving NHS time and resources on talking therapies, and keeping the economy growing. Pressure to return to work, always a problem for people experiencing stress but particularly noticeable coming out of lockdown, is driven by repressive human resources regulations—even in public services, despite individual managers often being aware of the difficulties for employees experiencing stress. Additionally, the use of these drugs further distorts the power relationship between doctors and patients.

Services

Mental health services, like all NHS services, were described by one participant as a 'shell', with little beyond waiting lists. Others pointed out that progress will be limited until the 10-minute guideline for GP appointments is changed. People experiencing mental distress need to be offered a choice among a wide range of specialist services. If we are to fight against quick-fix drug treatments, we must also advocate for fundamentally better-resourced and organised health services.

Going Forward

People will have been changed by what has happened, one participant suggested. They will change further as this epidemic and its social and economic impact continue to get tougher. They just won't accept going back to the previous 'normal.'

Another participant from Ireland pointed out that we've seen what authorities are capable of doing under pressure—

for example, the introduction of special supportive conditions for university students sitting exams remotely and housing homeless people in recently built houses, which have now become vacant because they are no longer affordable.

Covid-19 has highlighted just how many people are living with loneliness. We need to start a conversation about how we support people for whom social contact is essential.

In general, it was suggested, we should move forward and explore ways of addressing the experiences shared during this discussion. Most fundamentally, we should argue the point that 'safety' must include our mental as well as our physical safety.

Burnout

For my part, the discussion a month ago has left me more receptive to the mental state of people around me, as well as to my own. At the same time, there seems to be a new readiness among people I know or meet to speak in more depth about how they are feeling. The standard answer to "How are you?" is no longer just "Fine, thanks." One deeply committed activist friend in London told me he was taking a week's break—he felt "burnt-out." He was appalled by the quantity of death and suffering he'd witnessed. He said that at the start of the pandemic there had been so much energy and positive action. He'd felt swept up by it and optimistic. It really seemed possible to prevent the huge number of deaths and devastating economic impacts we all knew would flow from the Government's initial herd immunity strategy. But in the end, that energy and action had failed. And where, throughout this crisis, he asked, was the left? It just wasn't there— whether in parliament, parties, the unions, or at the front of protests. It was disheartening. He also said that there weren't many people he knew who weren't at or near the same level of distress that he was experiencing.

I found this helpful personally because I have had similar feelings. And I know that others have been driven to the edge through a wide range of personal battles—including, for example, delays in diagnosis or treatment of their cancer, as a result of the displacement by the epidemic of the already struggling NHS cancer services.

Lack of Confidence

Many trends in capitalist society, particularly over the last forty years, have undermined the confidence of working people. Marx's theory of capitalist society alienation, in which he most relevantly included alienation from each other and alienation from self, has held up. He did not foresee consumerism and appearances (or 'keeping up with the neighbours') as ways of expanding the internal market and at the same time weakening resistance by turning working people against each other—the particularly cunning and successful double trick which capitalism conjured in the 1970s (see Mike Leigh's brilliant satire *Abigail's Party*). Since the 1970s too, trade unions have been relentlessly sapped of their previous power. The confidence of both workers and communities is at an all-time low.

I'm old enough to remember my mother holding me back from being run over by Churchill's car. We were at the front of the crowd in Victoria Square, Birmingham, during the 1945 election campaign. The thing that most impressed me about this hero was the way he kept a cigar going in the back of an open limousine. But within a few weeks, people across Britain had rejected him. This was the beginning of one of the few times over the last 75 years when we came together, fighting collectively for better health and welfare. It helps to have experienced, even as a child, the spirit and successes of that time. By the 1960s, we were in retreat again and have been ever since, apart from a last burst of confidence in the late 1960s and early 1970s, snuffed out by Thatcher and the continuous succession of neoliberal governments ever since. Collective action, which both arises from confidence and builds it, has been stifled. Instead, we've been persuaded to consume goods, services, and information as individuals. On our own, we are left afraid—frightened by the virus, by the evidence of climate breakdown, closer to us now, and frightened by the prospect of unemployment and our powerlessness.

But Covid-19 is bringing a new wave of confidence in some communities and protest groups, for example, in North Edinburgh, as described recently on this site at https://www.rs21.org.uk/2020/08/25/interview-neighbourhood-organising-in-edinburgh/. This looks like the beginning of a movement that could spread from communities to workplaces, where the confidence of workers is being further eroded by the immediate threat of redundancies.

The opportunity

It does seem to some people that Covid-19 has held up a mirror not only to the deep flaws in our society but also to our shared humanity. Of all the things we should refuse to go back to, perhaps the most crucial for our survival is the version of humanity that has been distorted by capitalist society. The time is ripe. There is little doubt that what we are experiencing now is the bumpy ride through the end-stage of capitalism. Some economists are predicting that we are about to find ourselves in the worst world recession in 300 years. This is not only the opportunity of our lifetimes, but it's also the opportunity missed by all those in previous generations who fought for a better world, and the opportunity that the next generation will miss if we don't take it. How long the end-stage of capitalism lasts, and whether something better replaces it, is up to us, not as individuals but collectively.

Our mental health and confidence will be central to this fight. Our greatest resource in this respect may be talking with each other, listening more carefully, and expressing more openly how we feel. Yes, we should oppose the biomedical model of mental distress, and we should fight for whatever new services we discover can help us. But whatever services we win or don't win, we will have each other.

HEALTH SERVICES (7.11.17)

One night, a month ago, in the Californian city of Santa Rosa, which has a population of 175,000, more than a thousand homes were destroyed to their foundations in a firestorm. The pictures were described as "resembling the apocalypse Kim Jong-un keeps promising to bring to America." Over recent years, fires like this have become commonplace in California. The generally understood cause is climate-change-induced extreme weather events—unprecedented heavy winter rains growing the luxuriant mountain vegetation known as chaparral, which is then dried into crisp tinder and ignited by unprecedented pavement-melting summer temperatures. But what's generally ignored is the real estate juggernaut that continues to drive the suburbanisation of these inflammable wildlands—a juggernaut that, as has been said, "... confounds human intelligence ... and demonstrates the hopelessness of rational planning in a society based on real-estate capitalism."

Reading about this, I was struck by the parallel with the English NHS. In 2012, the Health and Social Care Act opened the door wide enough for another juggernaut to roll through and seek profit from providing NHS-funded clinical services. Scotland and Wales used their devolved powers to avoid this, but in England, the juggernaut was soon competing successfully with NHS Trusts for contracts. Robust arguments that health care cannot be commodified and at the same time improved were brushed aside. The overriding political priority for the Government was not to increase spending on the NHS. As a result, annual NHS budgets have flat-lined in real terms since 2010—despite population increases of around half a million annually and despite increased expenditure on new investigation and treatment opportunities.

However, something unexpected has happened. By the summer of 2016, it had become clear that the 2012 Act had comprehensively failed. Services were not being made more efficient but were being cut, and private companies were finding it increasingly difficult to turn a profit. There was simply too little money in the NHS pot. At first, the Government responded with a sudden switch to an unprecedented level of centralised command and control in the shape of Sustainability and Transformation Plans, using a smokescreen of jargon and complexity to get around the 2012 Act by stealth. But in its election manifesto this June, the Conservative Party admitted that the market model for the NHS is dead.

To appreciate the extent of panic in this party that this and other realities have triggered, we can look to some of the things said by senior members of the party at their conference last month:

Philip Hammond, on his visit to Cuba, curiously remarked, "I found cows in the field, but no milk in the shops ... That's what socialism does to a market ... It's all very sad," he said of Labour's shift to the left, "because for 35 years we had a broad consensus in British politics about our economic model ... As this model comes under renewed assault, we must not be afraid to defend it."

Boris Johnson: *"This battle of ideas is not lost in memories of the 1970s. It is back from the grave, its zombie fingers straining for the levers of power, and that is why we cannot rest."*

Theresa May: *"The free market remains the greatest agent of collective human progress ever created. So let us win this argument for a new generation and defend free and open markets with all our might. Because there has rarely been a time when the choice of futures for Britain has been so stark."*

And Eric Pickles, in his review of the Conservative Party's performance in this year's General Election, said: *"In my Whitehall office as a minister, over my left shoulder, facing visitors, was a photograph of Che Guevara. It was there to remind me that, without constant vigilance, the cigar-chomping Commies will take over once again."*

To borrow from the Prime Minister, I would say there has rarely been a time when the choice of futures, not just for Britain but for the world, has been so stark. And on the left, we need to grasp this opportunity by giving active support wherever we can to the gathering realisation that it's the juggernaut of capitalism itself we need to go for by the throat, rather than its diverse individual manifestations. More people, I think, are beginning to see common cause in their particular everyday miseries, whether it's a home destroyed by fire in Santa Rosa or West Kensington, arriving as a Sub-Saharan refugee in Libya and being packed back home, or being turned away by mental health services because your diagnosis doesn't fit their tariff. Are we seeing the beginnings of a mass movement, which, underpinned by common cause and participative democracy, could grow strong enough to stop the juggernaut in its tracks?

Failed health care internationally is likely to play a large part in this mix, for the simple reason that we are all patients. If we're not ill today, we know we could be next week. Illness is a fact of life. 660,000 people use the NHS every day. On top of that, NHS staff constitute 5% of the total workforce. So, I'd like to take this opportunity to share some thoughts about health services, illustrated by my personal experience, as a small contribution to the discussion about how we can prepare for a mass movement.

If we want a health service that is truly fairer, I suggest we base it on three principles. It should be a health service that:

1. Will be completely free to everyone, dependent only on need, with no opportunities to purchase an alternative service.

2. Will aim to maximise health, giving each individual the chance to enjoy the best possible life (in contrast to the capitalist priority of ensuring a surplus of people well enough to work).

3. Will be controlled by its workers in partnership with the people it serves.

This is much more than a return to 'the spirit of '45' in Britain. The original NHS was led by a political elite committed to reforming capitalism rather than overthrowing it. From the beginning, it was heavily contaminated by the vested interests of doctors, who were dragged kicking and screaming into the new NHS in 1948. As early as 1952, the lead principle of the NHS—that it should be free at the point of delivery— was eroded by the introduction of charges for prescriptions and dental treatment. From the beginning, people who were able to afford it could purchase private care, though their assumptions that payment gave them better care were not always correct.

After qualifying as a doctor in the '60s, my first NHS job included emergency cover for the patients in the private hospital across the road from the NHS hospital. The benefits these private patients received for their money were better food and seclusion in private rooms—otherwise, treatment in the two hospitals was identical.

I came to dread calls to see private patients, soon discovering that there weren't enough nurses to observe the patients adequately in their separate rooms. The Nightingale wards in the NHS hospital worked much better because all patients were visible from the nursing station—and if a patient in trouble wasn't immediately spotted by the nurses, the patient in the neighbouring bed could be relied on to give a shout down the ward.

Because of the delay in being called to emergencies in the private hospital, I often found myself arriving to find the patient in a life-threatening condition. Resuscitation in the cramped private rooms, which were less well-equipped with oxygen and defibrillators than the NHS wards, was a nightmare. I wasn't paid extra for the work in the private hospital—it was just assumed to be part of my NHS job. The consultant I worked under drove a Rolls-Royce.

I'd now like to suggest five specific improvements that we could consider incorporating into a new health service. These five suggestions emerged from my time working as a children's doctor in the NHS, as well as from listening to people in Cumbria who have felt able to talk to me as an ex-doctor over the 35 years since I quit my NHS job. They are an attempt to address what, in my view, are some of the worst flaws in our NHS today. I offer these suggestions for discussion and debate. It's not for me or anyone else to draw up a blueprint.

The first of these suggestions is that we need to find ways to **close the gap between general practice and hospital**.

During my time as a paediatrician in East Africa in the 1970s, it was common to see a pole slung five feet from the ground between two trees at the entrance to a rural clinic. Women in labour who could walk under the pole without ducking were admitted to the labour ward, based on the belief that there is a correlation between short stature and a small pelvis. Women who couldn't walk under the pole were turned away, as the labour ward had neither the space nor the staff to care for them.

How to select patients for special care—for example, admission to hospital—as opposed to simple treatment or no treatment is a significant organisational issue for any health service. Gradually, through my time as a doctor, I realised how poorly this is organised in the NHS.

After leaving the NHS and moving to a rural community in Cumbria, neighbours and friends in that community often phoned or came to see me for advice, knowing that I had been a doctor. Usually, it was because they were sure there was something seriously wrong with themselves or with a family member but hadn't been referred to hospital by their GP.

I remember Billy, for example, a 12-year-old with swollen neck glands, whose mother had taken him three times to their GP, each time being reassured that there was nothing serious to worry about. Sally was a 15-year-old with a three-day history of tummy pain, whose GP told her and her parents to wait and see. Ivy, an elderly (and wise) woman, had seen a TV programme about ovarian cancer and, from the symptoms described, thought she might have it. But over the previous two months, she had failed to get a succession of GPs to act.

I gave the same advice to all three of these people—go straight to the Accident and Emergency Department of the local hospital. They followed the advice, and all three were admitted. Billy was found to have leukaemia and recovered after a long course of treatment. Sally had a badly inflamed appendix removed the same day. Ivy was correct—she had ovarian cancer, which had become untreatable. These aren't isolated stories. I could tell many similar ones—about unnecessary suffering and even unnecessary death.

When there's so much talk of the importance of early diagnosis and treatment, why does late referral or non-referral to hospital continue to happen? From what I've heard from many patients, who have given me the privilege of sharing their experiences with me, combined with discussions with those doctors who will still speak to me, I see four reasons: under-resourced hospitals; power relations between GPs and hospital doctors; the sharp division of responsibility between these two groups of doctors; and an institutionalised lack of respect for patients' opinions about their illnesses.

As we all know, hospitals, along with all NHS services, have suffered from under-investment for a long time. Particularly disastrous have been the PFI experiment during the Blair years and the frozen NHS budgets under Cameron and May. One result of this is that junior hospital doctors responsible for deciding whether or not to admit patients referred to them by GPs have become increasingly anxious about admitting patients who might turn out not to have needed admission—an aversion to so-called 'unnecessary admission' which they consistently communicate to the GP when she phones to ask for a patient to be admitted. Accordingly, GPs think at least twice before requesting admission, not wanting to risk the ignominy of having their request rejected.

This fear on the part of GPs has been reinforced by their inferior power relationship with hospital doctors, which dates back a long way. When I was a medical student, the prevailing view in the NHS was that you ended up in General Practice only if you weren't good enough to become a hospital specialist. Despite strenuous attempts over the years to improve their status and remuneration, many GPs have never fully recovered from this sense of inferiority.

The sharp role delineation between hospital doctors and GPs doesn't help. The two rarely meet, except in the context of continuing education—usually in the form of hospital doctors educating GPs. GPs cease to have any say in their patients' management once they are admitted to hospital or are under specialist care as outpatients. There is also too little opportunity for GPs and hospital doctors to learn together from the mistakes, sometimes fatal, which result from late or non-referral.

In a small attempt to address the power relations between different NHS workers, in the late '70s I had the opportunity to set up a project in Newcastle called the Riverside Child Health Project. We based a team of children's doctors, health visitors, social workers, and community workers in two vacant school classrooms in the desperately deprived west end of the city. We worked as equals as much as possible, sharing the same open-plan office and cultivating mutual respect through close consultation. We also established arrangements with all local GPs for regular joint clinics, in which a children's doctor and a GP would see children together.

The essential feature of these sessions was that they were open, meaning parents could bring their child without an appointment—whether they thought the child was ill, weren't sure if the child was ill, were worried about the child's development or behaviour, or wanted to discuss family difficulties. These sessions were successful from the perspectives of both the families who attended and the GPs, so we extended the system to general practices in the east end of Newcastle.

In a fairer NHS, it will be natural for power relations to be addressed openly—not only between GPs and hospital doctors but also between all NHS workers, including those in non-clinical roles such as cleaners and porters, whose labour contributes to the provision of healthcare.

The second of my five suggestions is that we need to reduce the workloads of NHS workers. Speaking with junior hospital doctors last year during their protest, I realised that their workloads are not much different from mine 50 years ago.

As a first-year doctor in a large London hospital, I was on call for new admissions every other day, in addition to being responsible for the 50 patients already in my two wards. On these call days, we rarely finished our list of tasks before 3:00 in the morning, after which we were likely to be called out of bed at least once before getting back to the wards to start the next day's work at 8:00. We then worked another 12 hours before our night off. Meals on call days mainly consisted of cornflakes pilfered from the ward kitchen. One in three weekends was so-called 'off,' meaning we could leave around 2:00 on Saturday afternoon and had to be back on the ward by 6:00 on Sunday evening. After six months of this, I developed a bleeding ulcer and spent the next six weeks in bed on one of my wards.

We knew that, too often, we were too exhausted to be effective doctors and that, as a result, patients were suffering, sometimes even dying unnecessarily. But we felt powerless to change things, having been conditioned as students to be sycophants, giving ourselves up as burnt offerings to our consultants, the gods we aspired to join. Stepping out of line would have cost us the next six-month job and prejudiced our promotion.

Newly qualified doctors may work fewer hours than we did, but they describe an intense quality of work, driven by the explosion of new technology available for diagnosis and treatment over the past 50 years. Overall, their work is every bit as stressful as mine was, and this remains a live issue in terms of the Junior Doctors' dispute with the government.

The government's attempt to argue that weekend services can be improved without additional resources is a farce and an insult to the intelligence of the electorate. Their disrespect for the commitment of junior doctors is extreme arrogance, and their attempt to discredit them is a cynical and devious excuse for further privatisation. .

But now there's one significant difference from my day. The mass of junior doctors has learned and organised, and for the first time in history, they are identifying themselves as workers, not as gods. They are standing up for the NHS they believe in and for their patients, whom they care about deeply. Last year was a close call—they nearly brought the government down. Next time, with mass support from all of us, they might succeed. Their protest points the way toward a fairer health service, where all workers are respected for their contributions and given sufficient time off for rest and refreshment.

Junior hospital doctors have been brow-beaten for generations into believing that they will only become truly proficient through dedication to long hours of work. Counting hours, complaining about them, or expressing fatigue is frowned upon. We need to support these workers, who hold our lives in their hands, in breaking down this hierarchical myth and calling for more rotation of front-line responsibilities and greater sharing of responsibility among doctors, nurses, and other workers.

My third suggestion is that we need to decentralise the delivery of health services. Health issues and illness patterns vary significantly across different localities, even within this small country. NHS organisation has always paid too little attention to local needs. In recent years, the imbalance of power between Whitehall and local NHS services has allowed the centre to impose structural adjustment programmes on deficit-spending NHS Trusts, similar to those imposed by the EU and IMF on poor countries. The Success Regime for Cumbria is an example of such a government-imposed NHS structural adjustment program. The cost-cutting measures coming from Whitehall demonstrate no understanding of Cumbria's geography and completely fail to recognise that the root causes of the deficit are the low level of health across most of Cumbria, its scattered population, and insufficient funding.

The relationship between poor health—both mental and physical—and disadvantage in wealth, employment, housing, and services is well established. The poorest areas need a different, more collective approach to health and positive discrimination in the allocation of resources.

One of the aims of The Riverside Child Health Project in Newcastle was to provide additional resources in the poorest part of the city. This initiative was triggered by research showing that a disproportionate number of children's deaths and hospital admissions came from the west-end wards along the bank of the Tyne.

Three years into the project, we were able to demonstrate measurable benefits. Although the improvements in mortality and serious illness rates were small—understandably so given the massive economic and social challenges families continued to face at a time when capitalism was rampant in the city—our experiment showed that a team including expertise in medicine, preventive health, social work, and community development could work effectively. Notably, local people developed the confidence to contribute to our strategies and became active members of the team.

A fairer health service will not achieve health equality overnight. It will require a network of initiatives that positively discriminate for those most damaged, mentally and physically, by the capitalist system. We need to start discussing how these locally tailored services can be best delivered, drawing on experiences from other countries. For example, in Havana, every block has a doctor and a nurse who live in the block and share responsibility for its health.

The fourth of my five suggestions are that control of health services should be radically democratised. Given that health needs vary markedly between localities, it follows that health services should be locally controlled. Local residents and NHS workers will best understand what services are needed, so they should control their services in partnership.

Attempts to democratise the NHS have largely amounted to a catalogue of half-hearted or insincere initiatives, all of which have failed to halt the centralisation and erosion of democracy. Local Community Health Councils (CHCs), established in 1974 with much rhetoric about giving patients a new voice, exemplify this. As a member of a CHC in Newcastle in the late 70s, I worked alongside other committed volunteers. We visited hospitals and other services and held monthly meetings, which became increasingly lengthy. Despite our efforts, we never completed the meeting agendas, and our time was consumed by lengthy documents handed down from above. Without opportunities to address the issues raised by the impoverished patients I worked with, I resigned after two years of fruitless effort.

In 2003, the Government abolished Community Health Councils (CHCs) without discussion or explanation, to the dismay of many dedicated individuals who had served on them. CHCs were replaced by Public and Patient Involvement Forums (a name reflecting their lack of power). These were succeeded in 2008 by Local Involvement Networks, which in turn were replaced by Healthwatch in 2012—an attempt by the Government to further reduce resources. The frequent replacements and increasingly vague names of these bodies highlight their systemic failure. This failure was inevitable because all these initiatives were imposed from above by governments whose overriding priorities were to maintain power and minimise NHS spending, rather than improve public health.

A central aspect of the Riverside Child Health Project (RCHP) in Newcastle was to provide opportunities for small groups of parents to meet informally with a team member. In one such meeting, a group of six mothers shared their experiences of taking their children to the operating theatre for injuries, tonsillectomies, or suspected appendicitis. They described how their young children, many of whom were under five years old, were taken from them by a nurse in the corridor outside the anaesthetic room, crying and screaming as they were carried away. I wrote to a senior anaesthetist about this issue. After several initial rebuffs, he agreed to meet with the group of mothers at the Project. Confronted by their concerns, he agreed to change the policy, allowing parents to stay with their children until they were anaesthetised. The policy was subsequently revised.

A priority for a fairer health service should be the establishment of Neighbourhood Health Committees that are well-resourced, fully empowered, and elected by local residents and health workers.

Reclaiming Our Bodies

My final suggestion is the most fundamental: we should start to **reclaim our bodies**. The relationship between doctors and patients in the NHS embodies a fundamental contradiction to the principle that power should belong to the people. While some doctors excel at listening to their patients and involving them in decisions about their treatment, the overall trend favours doctors as the ultimate authorities on health. This dynamic has led us to view doctors as primarily responsible for our well-being. Rhetoric from governments and medical organisations about patient empowerment, as with many top-down initiatives, has only deepened the power imbalance between doctors and patients. The term 'patient', originally meaning someone who suffers, has come to signify passivity—someone under medical care.

Our experiences of birth and death have also been appropriated. The Caesarean section rate in the UK was 31 percent in 2019/20, despite evidence that maternal and newborn death rates do not improve beyond a rate of ten percent. In the USA, the rate is 32 percent. While death rates are one measure, there is no evidence that non-fatal birth outcomes for mothers and babies improve with higher rates of Caesarean sections. The women's movement of the 1970s and 1980s, which fought for reduced medical intervention in childbirth, has largely faded.

The situation with end-of-life care is more positive. Terminally ill patients and their families, despite facing significant challenges, have succeeded in emphasising that the quality of remaining life matters more than its length. Consequently, palliative care, guided by patients and their families, is improving. However, this progress is constrained by NHS austerity measures and remains dependent on voluntary contributions.

Yet, until we become terminally ill, we continue to view our illnesses as largely or exclusively the territory of doctors. This leads us to endure the often extraordinarily harmful side effects of the treatments they prescribe, a consequence of a medical model focussed on cure at all costs, driven by profit-hungry pharmaceutical companies.

Every illness is uniquely characterised by a particular body's resilience or vulnerability. Each case of the flu, appendicitis, or heart attack is different, presenting subtly different symptoms and progressing with varying severity.

One of the most useful things I was told as a medical student by an enlightened doctor was that the patient is their own best specialist. From this, I learned to ask patients early in the consultation what they thought was wrong with them. Nearly always, this resulted in the patient giving me useful information in reaching a diagnosis. Only once did a patient respond, 'That's your job, doctor.' When I began to specialise as a children's doctor, I learned that parents often have a strong intuition about what is wrong with their child—if they're given the space and respect to express their opinion. This is particularly important with young children, who can't localise pain or explain how they are feeling. The younger the child, the harder it can be to distinguish between a serious illness, such as meningitis, and a baby who happens to be sleepy at the point of consultation. But parents and caregivers usually know.

So, early in my time as a doctor, I became aware of the benefits of sharing both diagnostic and treatment decisions with patients or with the parents of young patients. I began to feel that the NHS gives too little recognition to this potential benefit and became interested in strategic possibilities for giving patients a larger share in decisions about their illnesses.

While still in the NHS, I conducted a small study with 44 new mothers, asking them to keep a diary of their baby's symptoms and their reactions over eight weeks. The babies were between 6 and 45 weeks old, and all were first babies. The diaries showed that the mothers made almost daily decisions about their baby's health, usually without seeking medical advice. There was no evidence that they failed to appreciate the severity of their baby's symptoms or failed to seek medical advice when needed. My respect for mothers' ability to recognise when their children are ill was reinforced.

After quitting my job as a children's doctor, I accepted an invitation to teach orthodox medicine to groups of mature students training to become homeopaths. The invitation came from a well-organised college that delivered an accredited qualification. The aim of including some orthodox medical training in the course was to equip students with diagnostic skills, particularly for serious and potentially life-threatening conditions, and to provide them with an understanding of the usual course of different illnesses. An outline of the orthodox medical treatment for each illness was included so that, once the students became practicing homeopaths, they could work closely with doctors.

For one day a month over two years, we covered the relevant anatomy, physiology, history-taking, physical examination, differential diagnosis, usual course, and orthodox medical management of all illnesses, excluding very rare conditions. With minor improvements based on feedback, I continued teaching groups of students this course for ten years.

Multiple-choice assessments showed that nearly all students had understood and retained the information and found it useful in their supervised practice with patients. This experience confirmed what I had suspected as a medical student—that it needn't take five full-time years to communicate the basics of medicine, especially given that we only truly began to learn about being responsible doctors through supervised practice once we were qualified. The homeopathic students were a special group, highly motivated, with most of them having previously graduated in teaching, social work, or other university courses. But I emerged from the experience confident that the most important elements of medical knowledge are straightforward and can be transferred to most people who want to learn.

Later, I had the opportunity to conduct further research into how people respond to their symptoms of illness, or the symptoms of their children, and how they use healthcare services. In this project, I worked alongside some experienced public health researchers. We collected in-depth information from parents of young children and people over 60 years old—two groups likely to be high users of health services. Our findings showed that the people we studied were good at recognising when they were seriously ill but often had an incomplete understanding of the exact significance of their symptoms. We decided we should explore training for the general public in recognising and dealing with illnesses.

So, with the help of an experienced health trainer, I designed a course of six two-hour workshops called "Dealing with Illnesses," and offered it to the rural community where I lived. Fifteen people signed up for the course, all of them women—eleven parents of young children, and four older individuals. We met one evening a week for six weeks and covered some common medical emergencies, some common childhood illnesses, and some longer-term illnesses. Specific illnesses were chosen by the participants at the start of each session. We used facilitated discussions to share experiences of the symptoms of each condition, and to discuss whether and when the participants had gone to the doctor or sought other advice.

Armed with positive feedback from the participants in the "Dealing with Illnesses" workshops, I approached a large general practice to suggest they might try something similar for their patients. The diversity of unconvincing reasons the doctors gave for declining the suggestion (litigation risk, time constraints, room-space constraints, etc.) suggested that the underlying reason was a reluctance to share their power.

I suggest that in moving forward toward a fairer health service, we should begin to build a network for training people in how to deal with their illnesses. It should start in schools and be promoted as an adult education option in workplaces and community neighbourhoods. The potential benefits to both people's health and health service efficiency could be huge, and it would be a revolutionary step in addressing power relationships.

FOOD (10.9.17)

It was busy in the community room at Kinning Park Community Centre on Thursday evening. Between 6:00 and 7:00, the kitchen fed about 70 of us at the weekly communal meal. We sat at two long tables—people from the neighbourhood, community activists, workers at the Community Centre (staff and volunteers), and a large band of asylum seekers, mostly from Latin America, though I sat next to two Iranians. The atmosphere was rich—in solidarity, diverse tongues, and excellent food—cooked and served by local people and asylum seekers into an international mix of dishes, with ingredients sourced from supermarket surplus. You pay what you want, anonymously.

Food is not only an everyday necessity, eaten three times a day by those of us who can afford it. What we eat fundamentally determines how healthy we are. And what we eat, how it's produced, and how it's distributed have huge impacts on the climate and nature.

Collective opportunity

Moreover, cooking and eating together provide collective opportunities. If you've never worked in a kitchen to provide a meal for a large number of people, I can tell you that it's an object lesson in sharing ideas, skills, and working as a team. It can be challenging but is also extremely rewarding.

Eating together, whether communally or in households or workplaces, is an opportunity to stop work, enjoy the food, and catch up with each other—even talk politics.

In a new, fairer society, every neighbourhood could feature a kitchen and dining area offering communal meals and food at neighbourhood meetings. Even the most difficult meetings can be transformed by good food.

Farming

The world's largest urban farm is set to open early next year in Paris—on a rooftop. It will cover an area equivalent to two-and-a-half football pitches and produce 1,000 kg of vegetables and fruit daily, using organic methods.

In a future, fairer Britain, the biggest shift in methods of producing food won't be just towards iconic rooftop projects, though we may want to include them in the mix. The big change will be that all forms of intensive farming will disappear once and for all. Intensive farming is a capitalist madness that wrecks our land, destroys our wildlife, and damages our climate. All land will be nationalised. The doors will be shut to those huge agribusinesses and food corporations. The passion and expertise we already have in Britain for growing good food in a good way—currently held back or strangled by the corporations—will blossom.

Ignore the claim that the world needs intensive farming to feed its growing population—it's another capitalist lie. If small-scale farmers are given access to enough land, water, credit, and equipment, their productivity per hectare and per unit of energy used is much higher than on intensive farms. What's more, in a world of adequately supported small-scale farming, we won't need to be vegan to stop world hunger and climate change. Small farmers respect their farm animals, and their methods reduce the amount of methane produced by cows. It's not the meat that counts; it's how the meat is farmed—and, above all, who controls the farming.

Famine

Another lie is that famines are caused by world food shortages. There has never been a famine in the capitalist era that was due to a shortage of food. In every case, there has been plenty of food, but it has been prevented from getting to the people who needed it. Modern famine is political.

The root cause of An Gorta Mór, the Great Irish Famine of 1845–49, was the displacement of Irish families from the best pastures, where they had raised milk cows for centuries. This good land was stolen by the imperial British to satisfy the increasing taste for beef in Britain and the increasing appetite for profit among British capitalists. Even in the worst years of the famine, large quantities of food, not only beef, continued to be exported from Ireland to Britain.

The Ukrainian word for their Great Famine in 1932 and 1933 is Holodomor. It means "killing by hunger." This famine was a racist genocide orchestrated by Stalin. The harvests were not bad in those years—the Ukrainians' crops were stolen to feed Russian workers.

The devastating famine in Sudan in 1998 was primarily the result of civil war. The Sudanese government, with the support of militias, deliberately deprived the Southern Sudanese people of the food they had grown for themselves.

Supermarkets

The fair distribution of food across the new Britain will be straightforward. Corporate supermarkets will become a memory, with their control over what we eat and what we pay for it replaced by Local Food Committees, which will regulate the stocking and prices in community-owned shops and eateries.

Baked Beans

Food is such an ever-present feature of our daily lives that we're quick to feel shame and anger when confronted with people who are regularly going hungry. I'll never feel the same again about a can of baked beans after seeing I, Daniel Blake. In the new, fairer world, the painful memory that hunger was a feature of the neoliberal world, even in rich countries, will drive us to continually work together to safeguard revolutionary gains and to keep moving forward toward a fairer world.

LAND (25.11.19)

The Duke of Westminster is 28. He owns more land in the UK than the Queen. As a result, he's the richest person under 30 in the world.

Now, the Duke wants to make the people of Cundy Street and Walden Street homeless so he can demolish their homes and build high-rise luxury flats on the land they live on. Many of them have lived there all their lives. And this is just around the corner from the seat of so-called democracy.

It's a familiar tale. So familiar has it become that we tend to forget that soaring house prices, rip-off rents, insecure tenancies, dilapidated and poorly insulated flats, and homelessness are all underpinned by the political decision to make land a commodity, exchanged for profit instead of used for the public good.

And yet, land is and has always been the source of our daily needs – shelter, heat, food, water, health. In a fair society, these will be seen and managed as universal human rights.

On top of these historic needs, we now, suddenly and urgently, have additional calls on land if we are to stop global warming and survive its escalating impacts. We need land, both dry land and the sea (best to think of land and sea as one entity), to generate a lot more renewable electricity. We need land for planting new forests to capture carbon, and for restoring and expanding old ones. We need land for the right sort of farming, which also captures carbon. We need land upstream of densely populated areas, managed specifically to prevent flooding. We need land to enhance habitats for birds, insects, plants, and animals – especially for the many species now facing extinction. And we need land for our children to play in and explore.

Scotland is fortunate. It has a diversity of land types and sea features well-suited to meeting all these needs. Rich soils for grain, fruit, and vegetables in the east and the Borders. Good grazing for cattle and sheep in the west. Land too poor or inaccessible for food production, which can be used for carbon capture, renewable electricity generation, and flood prevention. And some of the best seas and coastlines in the world for offshore wind generation and the development of wave and tidal energy. This diversity brings with it an exceptional variety of wildlife.

The people of Scotland have a long history of enjoying and respecting the beauty of the land they share with other species. In his book On the Other Side of Sorrow, James Hunter charts this appreciation over the 1,500 years for which we have written records. From Columba, the earliest of the Irish monks to arrive on Scotland's north-west coast in the 6th century, to the Scottish Gaelic poet Sorley MacLean (died 1996), the writings left behind show a consistently deep sympathy and admiration for wild nature.

As the Scottish independence movement grows and progresses, we can look back at this heritage with pride that isn't nationalistic, isn't a romance of kilts and bagpipes, but welcomes whoever comes to live in Scotland to do so with dignity, to share this heritage, and to contribute to it.

Given the importance of Scotland's land, in the past, present, and future, who should own it? Through the ages, the idea that land should be owned by any individual has been ridiculed – there has long been a movement demanding public ownership of land so that it can be 'a common treasury for all'. As we move towards a fairer society, democratically controlled public ownership of all land should be a top priority. How else can land be used for the public good? Nothing less will solve homelessness, fuel poverty, food insecurity, global warming, or the extinction of species, including our own.

Here's how Sorley MacLean put it, in English translation:

Beyond the lochs
of the blood of the children
of men
Beyond the frailty of the plain
and the labour of the mountain
Beyond poverty,
consumption, fever, agony
Beyond hardship, wrong,
tyranny, distress
Beyond misery, despair,
hatred, treachery
Beyond guilt and
Defilement
Watchful, heroic,

the Cuillin is seen
rising on the other side of
sorrow

TRANSPORT (10.11.19)

I'm on a London train out of Glasgow. At Carlisle, it begins to fill up – half-term in England. By Preston, it's rammed.

Across the corridor, there are two mothers travelling together, outnumbered by their four children, all under six. At my table, there's a mother with her 12-year-old daughter, whom I initially label as autistic but who turns out to be pleasantly self-contained, with a book as well as a phone. Fathers seem absent, or at least not sitting with their children.

Up and down the corridor, other parents and grandparents shuffle like refugees hoping to find a seat. The corridor's too narrow for them to pass without backing up and is awkwardly narrow for pushchairs. Eventually, they resign themselves to gridlock. Sometimes a passenger with a seat gives one of the refugees a spell in solidarity.

This piece is supposed to be about transport in a future, fairer Scotland, but this journey is making me realise how much we can usefully learn, as the capitalist system crumbles around us, about how NOT to organise society.

It's becoming widely accepted in Scotland that the privatisation of public transport has been a disaster. The call for free, publicly owned transport, launched by the Scottish Socialist Party back in 2007, grows more insistent. Notably, there's a new movement demanding Glasgow City Council set up a free transport system in time for COP26 in December next year, when some 30,000 people are expected to land in the city for the official meeting and perhaps 200,000 for the alternative one, including indigenous people from faraway places. What an opportunity for Glasgow to showcase its progressive response to the climate emergency! And what an opportunity for activists and trade unions to make a radical demand in a short time frame—entirely affordable for the Council if it factors in savings on road maintenance (virtually no cars travelling across the city), savings on health services (pollution slashed), and benefits to the city's economy (journey times shorter for everyone).

But this morning, I'm thinking especially about families travelling with young children on intercity trains—how these journeys could become a positive experience, not only a free one. We can start to plan less crowded seating, with room for young children to lie down; wide corridors; user-friendly toilets instead of the current Heath-Robinson and unhygienic messes provided by Richard Branson; healthy, affordable food options—or no food for sale at all, with passengers bringing their own picnics (even young children enjoy helping to make sandwiches); and intercom announcements that are useful and respectful instead of inane and infantilising. And of course, we won't be needing all those scandalous first-class carriages.

On the train home, we're stopped by floods at Stafford—4 inches of rain dumped on Wales in 24 hours. I've spent the day at a conference on the climate emergency, which concluded that the current crisis, which is ecological, financial, and political, is a unique and present opportunity for transformation. At Stafford station, there's chaos. We are 1,000 passengers disgorged from two trains simultaneously at 10:00 pm (the scheduled arrival time in Glasgow for my train). We find that Virgin has no plan for our forward travel. We are dispensable to Virgin, and this realisation breeds immediate solidarity. I find myself in a group of six, which checks that Virgin will refund taxi fares, then contacts a driver known to one of the groups to Preston and Penrith, I'm deposited in George Square, where I transfer to another taxi to take me home, while the remaining three passengers carry on to Edinburgh. I get home at 04:30.

Back to the future, it's easy to fall into pessimism about the apparent complexity and scale of organising society when we start trying to plan for any one sector, like transport. Thinking ahead about transport in isolation can fail to take account of the transformation of society overall. Instead, we should consider transport in the context of changes in work, housing, and industrial planning. In a publicly planned society, people will live nearer to their workplaces, and they will work fewer hours. Long journeys on crowded commuter trains and buses will be a thing of the past. Links between trams, trains, buses, and subways will be designed for the convenience of passengers, not for profit. Roads will be less congested—even the private car, the supreme capitalist icon, may disappear. Getting around will be quicker, easier, and free.

The sort of chaos I experienced at Stafford is going to become more and more familiar as the climate deteriorates and private companies compete more desperately for profit in a disintegrating economy. A privatised transport system can neither adapt to escalating climate change nor provide an integrated transport system that serves the exclusive interests of passengers. They are blindsided by profit.

Post-Script (2024):

My daughter wants to travel for a few days to Cornwall from Glasgow. The return fare by train is over £250. By air, it's £70! As long as this discrepancy exists, how will people choose to travel in the most sustainable way?

WORK (14.7.19)

What do we mean by "work"? This unassuming word punches well above its four-letter weight.

As Marx helped us understand, "work" includes any productive activity in which we consciously shape the world around us, whether it's our paid job, our unpaid primary occupation, or carried out during our so-called "leisure time." Raising our children, caring for our elderly relatives, growing flowers or food in our garden, stacking logs, painting the house, cooking, shopping for the disabled person up the street, are just as much examples of work as are the paid work of a baker, a care worker, a laboratory technician, a plumber, a teacher, a farmer, a bus driver, a refuse worker, a doctor, or a worker in a supermarket.

Work, as defined here, is as much a daily human need as food and water. It's the chief way we experience fulfilment in our lives. But work can also be profoundly alienating. It depends.

Arguably, the key thing that makes work fulfilling is that its product should be of benefit. Benefit to both human society and the planet. Some workers in the arms industry are currently demanding work suited to their skills that is beneficial rather than harmful. This demand isn't driven by the threat of job cuts, as it was at Lucas Aerospace in 1976, but because these workers have become more thoughtful about the impact of their products in human and planetary terms.

But however beneficial work is, it doesn't feel fulfilling if it isn't valued. When I visit my friend in an old people's home, I notice the resigned weariness of the carers, alongside the resigned weariness of the residents. Care workers, carrying out one of the most urgently necessary and highly skilled tasks in a society that for the first time in human history has more people aged over 65 than under 5, are paid a pittance.

Universal Basic Income is coming back into fashion on the left as a way of addressing low pay and the unpaid work which still largely falls to women. But UBI has dangers. There's confusion between idea and proposal. Moreover, the right has exploited this confusion by coming up with versions that, if you unpick them, are decidedly fascist. What the political 'scientist' Charles Murray wants is to finally abolish all welfare in the US, replacing it with an annual cheque to every adult for $10,000.

As with so many potentially good ideas for reform in any sector of society, there is a more fundamental danger. If reforms, especially seductive ones like UBI, are seen and fought for as ends in themselves, they are likely to fail and, worse, to distract us from the real challenge, which is to change power relations.

The version of the UBI idea which envisages an unconditional, regular cash payment to everyone, while retaining some existing benefits—for example, those for disabled people and their carers—could be turned into a specific demand worth fighting for, because it would significantly challenge power relations. It wouldn't by any means change everything that needs changing, but it would be a step in the right direction.

Important though the questions of pay, income, and product benefit are, more fundamental still is the question of workers being in control of their work. Not only in control of their pay, and being able to choose what they produce, but also in control of the hours and shifts they work, the health and safety of their workplace, the arrangements for sickness, maternity, paternity, and pensions, and for learning opportunities.

There are plenty of successful models for achieving this control—cooperatives, especially if networked as in the

Basque Mondragon model and in the ownership of wind turbines in Denmark; employee ownership; and public ownership at community, municipal, or state level.

ENERGY (12.3.23)

In the bad old years around the millennium, many of us were obsessed with the idea that we could halt global warming by turning off the light, putting on a jumper, riding a bike, and eating vegan. It was all our fault, so it was up to us to clean up our lifestyles. It was easy.

They were bad old years because not only were we completely wrong, but we'd been distracted for 10 years from the real task of building a mass climate movement—10 years we now realise we couldn't afford to waste.

Now that the climate crisis has escalated into an emergency, and we've come to realise that global warming can only be stopped by changing the economic system imposed on us, some of the ideas we had back then don't seem so silly. Not as ways of stopping global warming, but as ways of saving energy once we've succeeded in changing the economic system.

Saving energy will be one of the most urgent things we'll need to work at in the new society. Yes, Britain has exceptionally strong opportunities to generate renewable energy. But all the methods we have ready, or will develop, still have challenges to iron out. Reducing the energy, we need for heating, lighting, cooking, transport, and food production will be decisive for an effective and just transition from fossil fuels.

We know how to make these savings technically, and we've worked out that the necessary infrastructure costs are affordable in relation to improving the energy efficiency of all buildings, a free transport system, and non-intensively farmed food distributed locally.

We don't need to reduce our standard of living to deal effectively with climate change.

With one exception. It seems certain we'll have to forgo flying. None of the research into alternative fuels for planes that don't have knock-on devastating side effects (like displacing food production with biofuel crops) looks remotely capable of producing solutions in the time we have available. But in the fairer society we're fighting for, we'll have free international rail and bus services. And we'll be able to afford more journey time, because working hours will be fewer and annual leave longer. Consider the interest of stopping over in Florence on your way to Greece. But this will be a hard transition for people who have family living in Canada, Australia, and New Zealand. Whether the sailboats will perform as described in the novel The Ministry of the Future (2020) – time will tell.

Once we've completed the transition to renewables, energy-efficient buildings, and a free and fully electrified public transport system—each overseen by democratic public ownership with employees calling the shots—we're likely to see the widespread development of collective approaches to living, which will save further energy. Take housing and food production, for example.

Co-housing—communities of self-contained homes with shared internal and external spaces—kicked off in Denmark in the 60s, then in the Netherlands soon afterwards. In the UK, it didn't gain traction until the 90s, but there are currently 19 established co-housing communities in Britain, with another 60 in development. Development, however, involves a long and often unsuccessful struggle for community groups, primarily because of the price of land and associated mortgage difficulties. It's not even affordable for many people. But with land in public ownership and a truly democratic government, there will be no significant obstacles. Co-housing has huge positive implications for caring for the elderly, and for the care and nurture of children in a collective setting—as well as for energy generation and efficiency.

With collective food growing, we're on more familiar ground. Most allotment sites are collective—plots held and worked individually, but skills, plants, and harvests are freely shared. Community gardens can be inspiring places, whereas in others, the challenges of maintaining collective organisation in an individualist society result in fraught relationships and a mass of weeds. Some of the most productive collective gardens are those that include therapeutic aims for people with mental health issues or provide training and occupation for people with learning difficulties.

What all these collective models have in common is low energy use. Whether through organic regulation or agreed practice, they avoid the use of fertilisers, herbicides, and pesticides, all of which are energy-hungry in their manufacture and distribution. They don't use much machinery, and little or no energy is needed in distributing their produce because it's consumed locally.

Collective, energy-saving approaches will also be applied to food processing. Bread, the staple of every household, will be produced in community-owned neighbourhood bakeries. The French local boulangerie, persisting despite free market pressures, shows that neighbourhood baking works and has the additional social benefit of being an early morning meeting place. There's no reason why it shouldn't thrive under community ownership once we've fought free of the so-called free market.

NET ZERO (21.3.23)

"Net Zero" was defined at the 2015 Climate Summit in Paris as "a balance between anthropogenic emissions by sources and removals by sinks of greenhouse gases." For example, it would be acceptable to continue burning gas in power stations as long as all the carbon dioxide produced in the process is captured and permanently stored.

Net Zero was an attempt to translate the temperature target of "well below a two-degree rise above pre-industrial levels" into something countries could be held accountable for.

Since then, governments have rushed to announce long-term Net Zero emissions goals. The Climate Change Committee has also fully embraced the Net Zero concept— hardly surprising given that the members of the Committee are appointed by the UK and Devolved Governments.

As a result of these goals, billions of dollars have been invested in the research and development of low-carbon technologies, all of which face massive technological, economic, and land use challenges when implemented at scale.

The Net Zero concept emerged in 2013 in the run-up to the Paris Summit, against the backdrop of the collapse of the talks at Copenhagen in 2009. However well-intentioned the idea was, it's notable that it arose among a group of 30 lawyers, diplomats, financiers, and activists, who met at Glen House, a country estate in the Scottish Borders owned by a 'green' investment pioneer.

The current front-runner technology, which governments are pinning their hopes on, is "Carbon Capture with Storage" (CCS). This is defined as "a process in which a relatively pure stream of carbon dioxide (CO_2) from industrial and energy-related sources is separated (captured), conditioned, compressed, and transported to a storage location for long-term isolation from the atmosphere." The companies developing this technology are either the same companies that extract fossil fuels or are closely related to them financially.

CCS is an energy-hungry process and, as such, is not financially viable at scale for the companies experimenting with it. They are calling for government subsidies. In the US, extracted carbon dioxide has been used to facilitate pumping in oil wells—a process known as "Enhanced Oil Recovery"—to close the energy gap, make CCS more financially viable, and enable the big energy companies to continue extracting fossil fuels.

On four related counts, CCS is not in the interests of either people or the planet. First, it requires too much energy; second, it would need subsidizing by taxpayers; third, it would be controlled by giant corporations that already make obscene profits; and fourth, the development would be too slow to prevent catastrophic climate change.

In the UK, at Drax Power Station—the site recently of vigorous strike action by inadequately paid workers (see six-minute video at https://www.youtube.com/watch?v=YqddGDBcY_Y) —biomass is being burned and, from time to time, some of the emitted carbon is being captured in a process called Bioenergy and Carbon Capture (BECCS). A previous ScotE3 Briefing on BECCS Microsoft Word - Briefing 10.docx (wordpress.com) explains why this is a problematic idea—primarily because it would require huge areas of land to be planted with monoculture forests.

It's clear, then, that both Net Zero and the technologies that underpin it are meaningless greenwash, used to justify continued investment in fossil fuel extraction—an effective distraction from the urgent need to deliver sustained radical cuts to greenhouse gas emissions in a socially just way.

What's needed is Real Zero, not Net Zero. We have the technology to achieve this—we don't need new technology. This is what we need to do:

Phase out the extraction of fossil fuels, starting now

Invest in renewable energy

Invest in mass transport

Invest in insulating buildings

Oversee all this through a publicly owned and democratically controlled Energy Company so that the changes can be as fair as possible to workers and their communities.

BIRD FLU AND THE NATURE CRISIS (15.7.22)

Whatever the risk of spread to humans, as yet thought to be low, the current outbreak of the H5N8 variant of avian influenza is a tragedy for wild birds, particularly sea birds. H5N8 both spreads more readily and causes more lethal disease in birds than previous variants.

Every bird species is precious in itself. But some of the sea birds currently dying are already rare. For these this outbreak could result in extinction.

If anyone has any doubts about the extent of the tragedy they should watch this short RSPB video https://www. youtube.com/watch?v=ED7SeFRP9kg&t=17s

What the RSPB doesn't say, because large NGOs are restricted by the need to nurture their relationships with governments, is that the disgusting methods which a largely deregulated poultry industry continues to get away with are the cause of this world-scale disaster. The H5N8 outbreak is one more example of the results of commodification of food for profit, and of the increasingly reckless sacrifice of nature by big business in the context of end-stage capitalism.

The severe variant of the avian flu virus is just the latest genie which capitalism has helped to escape from the bottle. And as we've learned from the Covid pandemic, once viruses have escaped there's nothing a capitalist world is prepared to do to put them back. We're told we just have to live (or die) with them, as if there was no alternative.

But governments have to say things which give the appearance that they care. Westminster's Biosecurity Minister Lord Benyon said recently: "Our wild birds are facing exceptional pressures from avian flu this year and we have seen the tragic effect it has had – particularly on our seabird colonies. I very much share concerns about the impact avian influenza is likely to have on breeding populations of wild birds in the future, particularly those that nest in large numbers and represent some of our rarer species." But his actions to save wild birds are restricted to limited culls of commercial poultry and instructions to the public about not touching dead birds. Nothing about regulation of the poultry industry – because regulation is prohibited by his government's rule-book.

As many of these birds are only or at least primarily found in Scotland, regulation of the poultry industry is certainly something that the people of Scotland should be shouting about. Instead we go on obediently eating chicken because it's cheap.

The Nature Crisis is often side-lined, especially at times like the present when human beings are facing multiple crises. Exploitation of nature by man goes back to the Garden of Eden. But for the roughly two hundred years since the crescendo of industrialisation in the West, we've become more and more conditioned to the arrogant idea that other species are here only for our benefit – note Lord Benyon's "our wild birds" and "our rarer species", implying that we have some sort of ownership rights over wild birds. It's arguable that this arrogance in relation to other species is the most fundamental reason for the current mess humanity is in.

The Scottish Government's Biodiversity Strategy Consultation closed a few weeks ago. I had the privilege of working with the Friends of St. Fittick's Park, Aberdeen, to submit a contribution to the Consultation. Our submission told the remarkable story of the Park's restoration and enhanced biodiversity over recent years, while now the Park is under threat of industrial development at the hands of the all-powerful North Sea Oil and Gas Industry – see World-scale scandal in Aberdeen – Employment, Energy and Environment (scote3.net)

The submission goes on to point out that the Scottish Government, led by the Scottish National Party for 15 years, has presided over a range of policies which have driven the Nature Crisis the Government is now consulting about.

These policies have in common that they are designed to benefit wealthy people and are driven by profit. Some are entirely the Scottish Government's responsibility, others are through collusion with the UK Government. Unless these policies are radically reformed any attempts to address the Nature Crisis will fail, sooner rather than later. The policies which have been most crippling for nature include:

1. Land ownership

50% of Scotland's private rural land is owned by 432 individuals, mostly large estate-owners and industrial-scale farmers. As historian James Hunter has said: "Scotland continues to be stuck with the most concentrated, most inequitable, most unreformed and most undemocratic landownership system in the entire developed world". In addition nearly all public land is controlled by central or local government, not by local communities.

2. The sacrifice of biodiverse land for development

Weak regulation enables biodiverse land to be paved over for industrial or unaffordable housing development.

3. Farm subsidies

Huge sums of money continue to be paid to farmers, particularly large livestock farmers, to boost their profitability. Further money is paid to mostly large farmers and estate owners to improve biodiversity, but most of these people are primarily concerned with increasing their wealth, both profits and land values. Biodiversity is not often their primary motivation.

4. Bioenergy with carbon capture (BECCS)

The Scottish Government remains wedded to the concept of planting up huge areas of land with monoculture fast-growing trees, even to felling diverse forests to make way for these new plantations. The plan is to burn the timber from these new forests in power stations and deal with the carbon emitted by "Carbon Capture" – a process yet to be developed and tested at scale.

5. North Sea oil and gas extraction

The Scottish Government is also wedded to extracting every last drop of oil and gas from the North Sea. This has a negative impact on marine species, as well as fuelling both the Climate and the Cost of Living Crises.

6. A one-nation perspective

The Scottish Government's current proposals for addressing the nature emergency are an example of its tendency to think in terms of only one nation. Biodiversity has to be considered internationally. We should be thinking in terms of what Scotland can do to contribute to the efforts of other nations.

Places like St. Fittick's Park can help us shift our mind-set towards thinking in terms of every non-human species being important in its own right - not only those species which benefit humanity or those which are threatened by extinction.

If the Nature Crisis was brought centre-stage two benefits beyond enhanced biodiversity could follow. First, at least some of the many people who care strongly about nature, given information which would help them to recognise that profit for the wealthy is what drives the Nature, the Climate, and the Cost of Living Crises in common, would join the fight to stop North Sea oil and gas extraction, which is fundamental to all three crises in the UK and Scotland.

Second, young people and children are in general more and more aware of the devastation to nature they see around them. These are the people who will sustain the fight for a better world long after our time is up.

Children in particular tend to be alert to the nature around them. The younger the children, the closer they are to the ground to make observations that we may not notice. A few months ago, at an Open Day for the Strathblane Wildlife Sanctuary it was my pleasant job to lead tours of the site. For the first tour of the day ten pre-school children and ten parents turned up at the gate. The tour was led not by me but by the children, who ran ahead to point out lady-birds, slugs and molehills.

Our fight as adults at this crisis-torn stage of history must include ensuring that every child has the opportunity to explore wild land in their immediate neighbourhood.

THE FIGHT TO SAVE ST. FITTICK'S PARK (8.2.24)

One of the most important campaigns in Britain is the fight to save St. Fittick's Park (in Torry, Aberdeen) from industrial development. This campaign is significant because it addresses all five of the most pressing crises we face today: global warming, the nature crisis, inequality, health, and corrupt politicians.

St. Fittick's Park

Much loved by the residents of Torry, St. Fittick's Park has been a public green space for centuries. From the 1970s, the park became industrially polluted by the neighbouring industrial estate. In response, the Torry community raised £178,000 to improve the park and the East Tullos Burn, incorporating paths and playgrounds. The burn was naturalised with meanders, reedbeds, and wetlands. Volunteers, including local children, helped seed and plant a large area with wetland and wildflower plants and create an extensive woodland. Now, the award-winning park's wild beauty and biodiversity are enjoyed by children, families, and naturalists who travel to study the many plants, birds, amphibians, invertebrates, and mammals.

The Torry Community

The Torry Community, with its 10,000 residents, is one of the most neglected areas in Scotland. Much of the housing is of poor quality, and St. Fittick's Park is the last remaining green space. Torry is surrounded by a new industrial estate, a railway line, sewage works, landfill sites, a large incinerator, and one of the most polluted roads in Scotland. Health workers have compared health outcomes for the residents of Torry with those in the west end of Aberdeen, where residents have access to 15 acres of mature, riverside woodland and no industrialisation. They found a 13-year difference in life expectancy between these two areas.

The Threat

St. Fittick's Park is under threat from industrial development that would cover half of the Park with concrete. In the 2020 Local Development Plan, Aberdeen City Council, under pressure from the Port of Aberdeen, rezoned the Park as an 'opportunity zone' for a new Energy Transition Zone (ETZ). Moreover, the Scottish Government failed to intervene and plans to provide public funding for it. ETZ Ltd, created by business partners Ian Wood's ONE, the Port of Aberdeen, Scottish Enterprise, and Aberdeen City Council, plans to destroy a vast swathe of the Park. However, throughout the process, they have not publicly declared their exact goals for the Park.

The Campaign's Challenge

Campaigners argue that saving St. Fittick's Park represents a local example of the global threats we face today. Their research suggests that ETZ Ltd has roots in the Port of Aberdeen's ambition to diversify into property development as oil and gas reserves dwindle. It seems to the campaigners that developers view the land around the North Harbour as an opportunity for development and gentrification. The industrial partnership argues that North Harbour industries must be relocated to Torry. In short, it appears that our planning system continues to favour social elites over ordinary people. Campaigners believe that the industrialisation of St. Fittick's Park is not about energy transition but is an 'auld-fashioned land grab'!

A Just Transition for Torry

Scotland has high aspirations for biodiversity, energy transition, and democratic participation. If these aspirations were genuinely applied to Torry, ETZ Ltd would utilise vacant industrial land rather than concreting over an award-winning park. If Aberdeen City Council and ETZ Ltd were truly listening to the people of Torry, they would halt these unjust and risky business plans. Friends of St. Fittick's Park are not opposed to energy transition, but they believe it should not come at the cost of a community's park. Campaigners seek to protect St. Fittick's Park because it directly benefits both biodiversity and the physical and mental health of the Torry community. They demand a just energy transition led by visionaries who serve community interests rather than those of wealthy corporations.

ACHIEVING CHANGE (10.7.19)

On the morning after the General Election, I met a neighbour in the street. She said, "So now we know. We've got to do it ourselves."

The fact that we are unlikely to achieve the extent and speed of change we now need through governments has been firmly highlighted by the simultaneous failures of the UK General Election and COP 25 in Madrid.

By 'the failure of the UK General Election,' I mean much more than the fact that the wrong side won (wrong for many of the 44% of voters who voted Tory out of desperation, as well as the 56% who didn't).

I left the Labour Party in 1983, not because I was fed up with it, but because, after campaigning on doorsteps in Newcastle Central in the 1979 and 1983 elections, I was utterly disillusioned with what seemed to me a hopelessly inadequate democratic process. I concluded that the desperate conditions of the people of Scotswood and Benwell, where I was working, weren't going to improve through any UK government because these people didn't have a voice worth the name.

Now I see that it's not only the desperate who don't have a voice, but all of us, and that general elections have become even more of a sham than they were 40 years ago.

UK parliamentary elections are:

- **Not participative:** Debate is largely left to politicians and pundits, whose views are fed by television and other media to households and individuals, stifling opportunities for wider discussion. There's a hesitancy to talk politics outside the household – secrecy about one's political views has become an established ritual. The only opportunity people may get to share their views is with doorstep canvassers, a one-off opportunity at a time they haven't chosen.

- **Not proportional:** As demonstrated again in this election, where the Conservatives won a majority of 80 seats with 44% of the vote.

- **Too centralised:** Despite its size, Britain is one of the most centralised states in the world. Just 5% of all tax revenue is raised by local government – in France, it's nearly three times that.

- **Too infrequent:** The next chance for us to vote in a general election is unlikely to be before May 2024.

- **Not adequately backed by power to recall an elected member:** Before 2015, voters had no power at all to recall their MP. Under the Recall Act of 2015, this can only be initiated by a court sentence of the MP or by the House of Commons Committee on Standards, not by the constituents.

- **Compromised by misinformation:** Voters' primal emotions are increasingly exploited with half-truths or lies spread across social media, their messages amplified and targeted to specific audiences.

- **Commodified:** Treated as profitable entertainment for television and other media.

Historically, significant changes have never come through governments. They have only come through large numbers of people insisting on them. There were large numbers of people who got together in this election campaign - across Scotland, North East England, Merseyside, South Wales, Bristol, and London – standing defiant for their interests, hopes, and values, seeing through all the misinformation. Across the country, only an estimated 22% of people under 30 voted Tory. There were others in Cumbria, Grimsby, and the ex-mining towns of Nottinghamshire whose communities have been destroyed to such an extent that they clung to the false promises dangled by those responsible for their destruction. But not so long ago, all these communities, regardless of how they voted on December 12th, shared the same human values and hopes.

The day before the election, Corbyn landed in Govan at 7:30 am in the midwinter dark, a cold wind blowing up the Clyde. Among the two hundred or so people who turned out to see him, there was hope – tangible as they waited for him, strengthening as he spoke. He spoke of his pride to be standing where Mary Barbour had led the women of Govan in the rent strikes and where Jimmy Reid had inspired the shipyard work-in. He spoke of his commitment to eradicate child poverty, put more money in workers' pockets, scrap Universal Credit, prioritise climate change through a Green Industrial Revolution, end the housing crisis, and save the NHS from privatisation. Most effectively, he invited people to trust him – trust him to say what he meant and to act on what he said. He made it clear that personal abuse has no place in politics because it is fundamentally disrespectful of the democratic process.

I too got distracted by this election. As Corbyn spoke and the crowd cheered, I wondered whether this was the beginning of a Scottish Labour resurrection. Was it still possible we'd wake up the next day to a Labour Government? Were we at a historic moment of radical change, led by a mass movement and administered by a Corbyn government? Or were the people of Govan going to wake up to find themselves facing more of the same – the dilemma of whether to turn up the heating or buy food, eking out their cash until the arrival of the next inadequate work payment or so-called benefit, and sitting for long hours in an overworked A&E with a greeting bairn?

What we've really woken up to is the opportunity to finally put behind us the fantasy that governments can give us what we need. Climate movements, independence movements, movements to save the NHS, movements to end the housing crisis, movements to abolish Universal Credit, trade union movements, movements to welcome refugees and to stand against all discrimination, and solidarity movements for the peoples of Chile, Catalonia, Palestine, and many other places where people are rising up – these movements can readily grow into a single movement, coalescing around a succession of specific demands, as long as we insist collectively on achieving what we need and turn our backs on sham democracy.

THE FUTURE BRITAIN (10.7.19)

What sort of society do we want to be part of in future Britain?

This question can no longer be dismissed as utopian. There's no doubt that the current arrangements for organising society are fragmenting before our eyes as they fail to meet even the most basic needs of working people and address the escalating ecological crisis. It's time to actively discuss what we want to put in their place.

Not just what we hope for, but what we can collectively fight for. If we don't begin to discuss what a better society will look like, and what we want to fight for, we could wake up to find that even worse arrangements have drifted into the vacuum.

How will work be organised and rewarded? What about the new benefits system we'll need? What will the new health service look like? Do we want a different approach to education? How can food production and distribution be remodelled so that everyone has access to affordable, healthy food? What arrangements will we put in place for energy production and distribution so that Britain responds quickly and comprehensively to escalating climate change, and so that fuel poverty is abolished? What about housing? What about public transport? And the big question of land ownership, pressing ever more urgently to be squarely addressed and resolved, particularly but not only in the Scottish Highlands?

I will suggest four key principles which cut across all these questions.

I had the opportunity recently on a long train journey to talk with a young woman from Albania who moved to the UK about ten years ago. She was with her English husband and their responsive nine-month-old baby girl, who played on the table between us. Aged nine when communism fell in Albania in 1991, she spoke warmly of the collective activities she and all the children in her community took part in after school – particularly helping on farms and with litter clear-ups. These sessions were fun and, more importantly, made her feel she was playing a useful part in her community. When she returns nowadays to visit relatives, she finds what she describes as "a complete loss of community." "OK," she said, "There were some things we didn't have, such as the freedoms to choose a job and where to live. But you were given a job and a house, so there was nothing to worry about."

This is not to idealise previous communist society in Albania. But this story of collective activity brought home to me once again the scarcity and small scale of collective opportunities in today's Britain. Yet people often grasp these few opportunities enthusiastically, suggesting perhaps that, at whatever level of awareness, they feel starved of collective action.

In the street where I live, two winters ago, people turned out from every house to help clear the snow dumped by the Beast from the East. For some of them, it was the first time they'd met each other. Long after the roadway had been cleared, they leaned on their shovels talking, then set to on the paths leading to everyone's front doors.

Random activities like this are a long way from established collective forms of organisation, but I suggest they demonstrate that an instinct for doing things together is alive and well, and that people working together become resourceful and efficient to an extent we've come to see as surprising.

Secondly, if collective organisation is one of the key cross-cutting principles on which to base a new society in Britain, then another one, closely related, is democracy. But let's call it new democracy, as our current version of democracy has become so distorted and dysfunctional that it's now widely recognised as an obsolete irony. The new democracy, permeating the organisation of both production and services, will be highly participative and local, with delegation to the center restricted to the minimum necessary. Delegates will be required to justify their privilege frequently and be subject to immediate recall.

A third principle of future British society, I suggest, will be an active commitment to an international perspective. We've learned through history, often bitterly, that a fairer society cannot work if it's restricted to one part of the world, at least not without becoming disfigured beyond recognition. The goal, to be kept constantly in view however ultimate, is a global fairer society. In practice, this means keeping active links with other parts of the world, particularly places where people are rising up or are under counter-revolutionary attack.

Fourthly and lastly, I suggest it's essential that we reject all blueprints – detailed plans stretching too far into the future. At times of change, new and unexpected forms of organisation constantly emerge. If we attempt to plan too far ahead and institutionalise too much detail, we're liable to become blinkered from the surge of human creativity which suddenly becomes available in a changing society.

We start with three strengths: there are many of us who want change and relatively few who resist it; we have the option to withdraw our labour collectively; and we can bring the current system to a halt by occupying the streets and key buildings. In the context of a highly infectious viral epidemic, mass street protest isn't possible. Knowing this makes our rulers more confident that they can stay in control. But we're developing and can continue to develop new, safe ways to take over the streets involving fewer, spatially distanced, disciplined protestors. These methods can be visually effective and at the same time challenge traditional methods of police control.

Our strongest weapon is to withdraw our labour collectively, walking out from workplaces that are unsafe or where the product isn't essential. It's encouraging to see that many teachers in England are currently preparing to defy the

UK government by not going back to school the first week of the year. Workers, communities, unions, campaigners, and marginalised people are coming together as never before.

Something unexpected often happens at times of instability, sparking a major uprising of the forces for change. We don't know when or what that will be, but when it comes, we need to be ready to describe clearly the world we want.

Vision

The story we need to get us through the Covid-19 pandemic is a story based on fairness, trust, knowledge, alleviation of poverty, better and new public services, worthwhile jobs, the right training and education, reducing carbon emissions, safe green places to meet in, participative democracy, and organising together to build and win the power to force policies for keeping each other safe from the virus.

It's the same story that we need to describe the world we want to live in and the world we want to leave for our children. A world where we have reduced inequality to the minimum possible, abolished poverty and racism, slowed down global warming to a level that will still be difficult but not catastrophic, and where we've come to a new respect for nature. A world where families can choose how many jobs they want between them and the jobs they want, rather than being forced to take badly paid and insecure work that doesn't interest them. A world where we trust each other, trust our elected representatives, have our say, and know that our say will count.

THE NEXT SEVENTY YEARS (12.4.18)

Those of our children and grandchildren who survive the next 70 years will have done so only through collective action, whether chosen or forced upon them by their material circumstances. They will have come to regard home ownership and private transport as obsolete; the rearing of children by both parents as irreplaceable; employment that by its nature or duration prevents mothers and fathers from raising their children as unacceptable; dogs and horses not as pets, but as partners contributing to the household or community economy; and the selfie as a symbolic aberration no less perverted than flashing.

Since a world in which private property no longer exists will be forced upon us, we had better start preparing for it, whatever our political persuasions. We can look for ways to distribute what wealth we have to those who need it, rather than hoarding it for our children, who will not be able to buy themselves out of trouble. We can begin to share what knowledge and skills we have with anyone wanting to acquire them, rather than guarding them as the preserve of our profession. We can care about others going through hard times, and if necessary, care for them. Alone, we can walk through the woods, over the hills, and by the sea, watching and learning about the world beyond humanity. Together, we can make music and dance.

Whatever our scepticism about the nature of human beings, we had better respect and trust each other. The next 70 years will reveal whether or not the human species is fundamentally decent.

POST-SCRIPT (2024)

When I wrote these pieces, I had a limited conception that it was the big corporations which call the shots. We must always bear in mind what we're up against. I've learned about the North Sea Oil and Gas Industry from my involvement in the campaign to save St. Fittick's Park. And I've learned about the Arms Industry through the continuing genocide in Gaza.

it's 3:23 in the morning
and I'm awake
because my great great grandchildren
ask me in dreams
what did you do while the planet was plundered?
what did you do when the earth was unravelling?
surely you did something
when the seasons started failing?
as the mammals, reptiles, birds were all dying?
did you fill the streets with protest
when democracy was stolen?
what did you do
once
you
knew?

(from *hieroglyphic stairway* by Drew Dellinger)

Milton Keynes UK
Ingram Content Group UK Ltd.
UKHW022021281124
451769UK00013B/287

9 781835 383551